Contents

Why Money?............................page **5**

Chapter 1 ....page **6**
The Story of Money

Chapter 2 ....page **11**
Earning Money

Chapter 3................................page **18**
Saving Money

Chapter 4 ....page **23**
Making and Using a Budget

Chapter 5 ....page **26**
Kids Take Action

Glossary..................................page **31**

Index ....page **32**

Kids
Manage Money

Ellen Keller

PICTURE CREDITS
Cover (foreground clockwise from left) © 1993 Mugshots/The Stock Market, Lloyd Wolf Photography, Arlington, VA, © John Terence Turner/ FPG, Sean Justice/Image Bank; (background left to right) © Stephen Frisch/Stock Boston Inc./PictureQuest, © Bob Daemmrich/ Stock Boston/PictureQuest; page 1 Ian Shaw/Stone; page 3 Don Smetzer/ Stone, (left inset) Doug Armand/Stone, (center inset) Howard Kingsnorth/ Stone, (right inset) Catherine Ursillo/© Folio, Inc.; pages 4-5,15 David Young Wolff/Stone; pages 5, 7 (bottom), 8 (right), 9 (bottom), 15, 28 Photodisc; page 5 (inset) Annabel Braithwaite/FPG; page 6 Thedor de Bry, America; page 7 (top) Photo by Mark S. Sexton, Peabody & Essex Museum, Salem, MA; pages 7 (center left), 12 (2) The Granger Collection, NY; pages 7 (center, right),18, 30 Superstock; page 8 (top) Picture Research Consultants Inc. & Archives, Topsfield, MA; (bottom) James Stanfield/National Geographic Society, Image Collection; page 9 Lisette Le Bon/Superstock; page 10 © Michael Krasowitz/FPG; page 11 Stephen Simpson/FPG; page 12(bottom) Dan Bosler/Stone; page 13 © Bob Daemmrich/Stock Boston/PictureQuest; page 14 Kindra Clineff/ Stone; page 16 (top) © Dennis MacDonald/PhotoEdit; (bottom) © Michael Newman/PhotoEdit; page 17 Sean Justice/Image Bank; page 19 Chip Henderson/Stone; page 20 (left) Andy Sacks/Stone; page 20 (right) Courtesy Andrew Collins; page 21 (left) Paul H. Henning/© Pictor; page 21 (inset) © Pictor; page 22 © Jim Cummins/FPG; page 23 © Ron Chapple/FPG; page 24 Lawrence Migdale/Photo Researchers, Inc., NY; page 26 © 93 Mugshots/The Stock Market; page 27 © Joseph Sohm/ Chromo Sohm, Inc./CORBIS; page 27 (inset) Bob Daemmrich/© Pictor; page 29 Lloyd Wolf Photography, Arlington, VA; back cover Deborah Davis/PhotoEdit, Myrleen Cate/Stone, VCG/FPG, Ken Chernus/FPG, Howard Kingsnorth/Stone

Produced through the worldwide resources of the National Geographic Society, John M. Fahey, Jr., President and Chief Executive Officer; Gilbert M. Grosvenor, Chairman of the Board; Nina D. Hoffman, Executive Vice President and President, Books and Education Publishing Group

PREPARED BY NATIONAL GEOGRAPHIC SCHOOL PUBLISHING
Ericka Markman, Senior Vice President and President Children's Books and Education Publishing Group; Steve Mico, Vice President, Editorial Director; Marianne Hiland, Executive Editor; Anita Schwartz, Project Editor; Tara Peterson, Editorial Assistant; Jim Hiscott, Design Manager; Linda McKnight, Art Director; Diana Bourdrez, Anne Whittle, Photo Research; Matt Wascavage, Manager of Publishing Services; Sean Philpotts, Production Manager; Jane Ponton, Production Artist.

MANUFACTURING AND QUALITY MANAGEMENT
Christopher A. Liedel, Chief Financial Officer; Phillip L. Schlosser, Director; Clifton M. Brown III, Manager.

PROGRAM DEVELOPMENT
Gare Thompson Associates, Inc.

BOOK DESIGN
3r1 Group

Published by the National Geographic Society
1145 17th Street, N.W.
Washington, D.C. 20036-4688

ISBN: 0-7922-8694-4

Seventh Printing June, 2018
Printed in the United States of America.

Why Money?

We all need money to pay for the things we need and want. We need money to pay for **goods** such as food and clothes. We need money to pay for **services** like getting a haircut or going to the doctor.

Think of all the different things you and your family spend money on.

- rent or house payments
- telephone
- electricity
- food
- car payments and gas
- bus, train, and plane fares
- cable TV, video rentals
- movies, games, and other entertainment

What did people do before there was money?

The Story of Money

Long ago, people did not need money. People hunted for food. They gathered wild berries and other plants. They made clothes from animal skins. They found shelter.

As time passed, people settled in villages. They planted crops and made what they needed. Sometimes, families produced more than they needed. They started to **barter**, or trade, with other families. One family might grow extra rice and exchange the rice for a cow they needed. Later, people began using money as a means of exchange. However, it was not the kind of money you use today.

What did European explorers and Native Americans use as "money"?

Goods as Money

Early people used different items as a form of money to "pay" for a product or a service.

- shells and whales' teeth
- strings of beads called wampum
- jewels
- rice and salt
- cattle and oxen
- large stones
- furs and dried fish
- gold nuggets

What do these items tell you about the people who used them as money and how they lived?

Coins and Paper

During the 600s B.C., people in the ancient kingdom of Lydia began using coins. The coins had a lion's head stamped on them to show that the king of Lydia had given them a guaranteed value. Traders soon found that coins were easier to handle than goods and lasted a long time. Later, other countries began to make their own coins.

The Chinese were the first to use paper money, probably as early as A.D. 600s. The Italian explorer Marco Polo saw the Chinese using paper money when he visited China in the 1200s. However, it took some time for European countries to see the value of using paper money. They didn't start using paper until the 1600s.

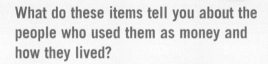

Money Through the Ages

- In 2500 B.C., the people of Babylon used clay tablets for money. These tablets were used like the checks we write today.
- Before refrigeration, salt was highly prized for cooking and preserving meat. Bars of salt became a form of money. Many people who lived by the ocean traded salt for goods.
- Native Americans used beads made of clam shells as money. The beads, called wampum, were strung together in patterns representing different villages. European explorers and settlers also used wampum to trade with Native Americans and each other.

Today, only governments issue money. In our country, the United States Mint makes all the coins. These coins are made of a mixture of copper, nickel, and silver. The Bureau of Engraving and Printing designs and prints the paper money we use.

What other kinds of money do people use today?

Money Today

Today, we have many ways to pay for things. We don't use only coins or paper money. Often, people prefer to pay for things with checks or credit cards. Paying with a check or credit card is easier and safer than carrying around a lot of "real" money.

Paying With a Check

A **check** is a substitute for cash. Checks are used in two main ways: to pay for things or as payment for work. People write checks to pay bills. People receive paychecks when they work.

How a Check Works

Suppose you have $100 in a bank checking account. You owe someone $20. You write that person a check for $20. That person will take your check to a bank to get the cash.

Your bank will pay the $20 to the other person's bank. Now you have $80 left in your checking account.

> Your name and address

> The person or store you are paying

> Today's date

Chris Jeffries
123 Main Street
Alexandria, Virginia 12345

100

DATE April 3, 2001

PAY TO THE ORDER OF   Ike and Mike's Bikes and Trikes $ 241.12

Two hundred forty one and _____ $\frac{12}{100}$ DOLLARS

MEMO   new bike

Chris Jeffries

> Amount of money you are paying

> Your signature

Paying With a Credit Card

The Flatbush National Bank in Brooklyn, New York, issued the first **credit** cards. Only bank customers could use the credit card at two or three different stores near the bank. Today, people use credit cards to buy almost anything, and they use them almost anywhere in the world!

Paying with a credit card is really borrowing money from a credit card company. Before a company, bank, or store lets you charge items on its credit card, it will check up on you.

The company wants to be sure you pay your bills. Then it will issue you a credit card. You have to be 18 before you can get a credit card in your own name.

Here's how a credit card works. Imagine that you are shopping for school supplies with your mom. When you're ready to pay for your supplies, your mom gives the salesperson a credit card.

The credit card company pays the store where you **charged** your school supplies. Your mom now owes the credit card company for the school supplies you charged. She can pay all of what she owes at the end of the month or she can pay the **minimum,** or only a small part, of the bill. If she does not pay the full amount that she owes, she must pay **interest.** Interest is an extra charge you must pay for borrowing money.

A Word About MONEY

The word *credit* comes from the Latin word **creditus** which means "to trust." So when someone gives you credit, it means that they trust you.

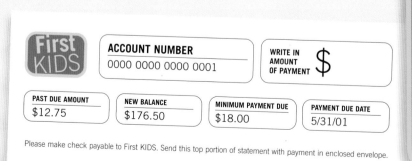

First KIDS	**ACCOUNT NUMBER** 0000 0000 0000 0001		**WRITE IN AMOUNT OF PAYMENT** $
PAST DUE AMOUNT $12.75	**NEW BALANCE** $176.50	**MINIMUM PAYMENT DUE** $18.00	**PAYMENT DUE DATE** 5/31/01

Please make check payable to First KIDS. Send this top portion of statement with payment in enclosed envelope.

CHAPTER 2

Earning Money

Throughout history, children have worked. Some children earned money to help their families. Some children earned money to buy things that they needed or wanted.

Today, children earn or get money in many different ways.

- receiving a gift
- getting an **allowance**
- doing chores at home
- performing a service, such as baby-sitting
- making and selling goods

What are some ways kids earned money in the past?

Kids at Work

Long ago, children often had jobs. There were no laws to protect them. Children worked long hours at hard jobs. They worked in unsafe and unhealthy places. They earned very little money for their hard work.

Some children sold newspapers on city street corners. These kids were called "newsies." Many of them were orphans. Their jobs helped to pay for their room and food. Other children worked in mines, at home, or in factories. Many worked in the **textile** industry, making clothes by hand. They were paid not by the hour, but for each item they finished.

Today, there are laws regulating child labor. You have to be 16 or over to work. Children ages 14 and 15 are allowed to work, but in a limited number of jobs. They can only work outside of school hours.

Getting an Allowance

An allowance is an amount of money given to children regularly by an older person. Some people believe that children should get an allowance. Others do not.

Some children do chores at home to earn their allowance. They might clean their room or take out the trash. Other children are paid an allowance whether or not they do any jobs at home.

Getting an allowance is a good way for you to learn to **budget,** or plan, what to do with your money. Allowances help you plan ahead. Since you get the same amount of money each time, you can plan how best to use it. You can decide whether to save or to spend your money.

What are some other ways kids can earn money?

Starting a Business

One way to earn money is to start your own business. You can have fun, earn extra cash, and learn lessons in responsibility. You can earn money doing odd jobs and by helping others.

Starting a Service-Oriented Business

You can run a business that offers a service. A service is a job or task that you do for people. Your customers pay you for the service that you do for them.

Here are some service jobs you might consider.
- mowing lawns
- shoveling snow
- washing cars
- baby-sitting
- delivering newspapers
- running errands for the elderly
- reading aloud to people
- tutoring younger children
- walking dogs and feeding cats

for Working
- Arrive on time.
- Agree on a price before you begin work.
- Ask if there are any directions you need to follow or anything you should be aware of. Be specific about what you have to do.
- Be polite.
- Check that your customer is satisfied with your work.

✓ Tips

for Making an Ad or Poster

- Describe the service you offer.
- Explain how and when to contact you.
- Tell why people should hire you.

Once you decide on a service that you'd like to do to earn money, you will need to advertise your service.

- Make a poster or flyer. Put it on a community bulletin board in the library, post office, or local market.
- Take out an ad in your local newspaper.
- Talk to neighbors and friends. They might need your service.
- Ask your customers to recommend you to others. Word of mouth, or good referrals, is a great way to build your business. One satisfied customer can lead you to more customers.

What if I like to make things? How do I go about selling things that I make?

Car Washing

By dependable and reliable students

Regular Brushless Wash

which includes:

- Vacuuming
- Windows Cleaned
- 100% Soft Cloth Wash
- Towel Wipe Down

Call Chris at (215) 555-2750 after school and on weekends.

$5.00

Starting a Product-Oriented Business

You might prefer to start a business in which you make something to sell. Before you do, here are some things you need to ask yourself.

- What kinds of things do I enjoy making?
- Do people really need or want any of these products?
- How much time during the week and on weekends would I have to make things? Is that enough time?
- What supplies will I need to begin? How much will these supplies cost?
- How much will people pay for what I want to make? Can I make money selling my product?

Here are some popular items kids have made and sold to earn money.

- greeting cards, wrapping paper, and stationery
- frames for photos or art work
- hair ornaments
- baked goods
- a community newsletter that sells ads
- simple jewelry
- nature crafts

for Creating Great Products

- Try to make your product different or special. This is what will convince people to buy it.
- Make two or three prototypes, or samples, first. Make sure your idea really works.
- Use the best quality materials. You want your product to last.
- Do your best work. Take your time.

for Pricing

- See how other products like yours are priced. This will give you an idea of what you can charge.
- Decide how much you will charge for each item. Then add up all the costs of your materials plus the time you take to create your product. Then add on a profit. The profit is how much you make after you subtract all your costs, including the cost of your time.
- Sell the product at a competitive and fair price.

for Selling

Where you sell your products is important. Here are places you might try to sell your products.

- community craft fairs
- school fairs
- local festivals
- church bazaars
- local stores

CHAPTER 3

Saving Money

As long as people have been using money, they have also been saving it. Long ago, people used to hide their money. They hid money under a mattress, in a sock, or in a drawer. Do you have a safe place where you keep your money? Maybe you keep your money in a piggy bank.

Where you save your money often depends on what you are saving for. If you're saving to buy a CD or to go to a concert, then you probably keep your money somewhere in your room.

If you're saving for a big purchase like a mountain bike or a school trip, where would you save your money?

Where should I save my money?

A Word About MONEY

People used to keep a pot made out of pygg, an inexpensive clay, around the house. They began to put their extra change in it. It became known as a pygg bank. Later, children's banks were made from other materials. But they were still called piggy banks.

Saving Money In a Bank

for Choosing a Bank

One place to save money is the bank. Putting your money in a **savings account** will help your money earn more money. If you put your money in a piggy bank, one year later you'll still have the same amount of money you put in. If you put your money in a savings account, one year later, you'll have more money than you put in. Why?

When you keep your money in a bank, your money earns interest. Interest is the amount of money a bank pays you to use your money. The bank uses your money (and the money of other people, too) to loan money to people and businesses.

The bank will send you a **statement** several times a year. A bank statement tells you how much money is in your account. It also tells you how much interest you have earned. If you leave your money in the bank, you can watch it grow!

Are there other ways to save money?

- Ask about a bank's interest rate. Different banks pay different rates.
- Ask about a bank's service charges. You don't want to pay for services you won't use.
- Look for a bank in your neighborhood. You want a bank that is convenient to use. Check the bank's hours. Is it open before or after school hours, or on Saturdays?
- Make sure that you have a savings account that lets you withdraw your money whenever you want.
- Check if the people working in the bank are helpful. You want to be able to get answers to your questions. Remember, it's your money!

Buying a Certificate of Deposit (CD)

Another way you can save money is to buy a **certificate of deposit** or CD. If you have some money that you don't need to use for a long time, this is a good way to make your money grow.

You can buy a CD at a bank. You agree not to use the money for a certain period of time. That period might be from six months to five years. You can't touch your money during that time. If you do, you must pay a **penalty,** or fee.

Since the bank is using your money for that time period, it will pay you interest. You will earn more interest with a CD than in a savings account. Can you guess why? It's because you promise to leave your money in the bank for a certain period of time. Banks pay different rates of interest. So, you may want to compare rates in newspaper ads before buying a CD.

Savings Bonds

Another way to save money is to buy a **savings bond.** You can buy a savings bond from the United States government. Bonds are a good way to save money. Here's why. You can buy a $50 bond for $25. Then you must wait 17 years until the bond **matures.** That means it has reached its full value of $50.

If you cash it before it matures, it will be worth less than $50. People sometimes give children savings bonds as gifts.

Investing in Stocks

You can make money by buying **stocks.** Stocks are shares in a company. Lots of kids invest in stocks with a parent's help. If you buy stocks, you are buying a very small part of a company. If your company does well, then your stock usually goes up. You make money. If your company does poorly, then your stock usually goes down. You lose money.

Some kids like to own stock, especially if the company makes something they like or use, such as computers, games, or clothes. You can find out how a stock is doing in the daily newspaper. The prices of most stocks are listed there.

If you sell your stock for more than you paid for it, you've made money. If you sell your stock for less than you paid for it, you've lost money.

Some schools have after-school programs that let students form a stock club. The kids select stocks and manage their **portfolios,** or group of different stocks. They have a contest to see who picks the best stocks and makes the most money. Of course, the money they **invested,** spent, lost, or made is just on paper. However, it is still a great way to learn about stocks. Often local companies that manage stocks for people will come to a school and help the club set up their portfolios.

Trading stocks on the floor of the New York Stock Exchange

Saving For a Short-Term Goal

Let's say that you want to save for a new bike. The bike costs $250. You know that you can earn $50 a month. You think you'll be able to save $25 or $30 of the $50 each month. Where should you put your money?

A savings account might be a good place. If the money is in a bank, you won't be tempted to spend it. Putting your money in a savings account will let you earn a little interest on the money saved. Also, when you take the money out, you will not have to pay a penalty for withdrawing the money. Try not to take the money out before the date the bank pays interest.

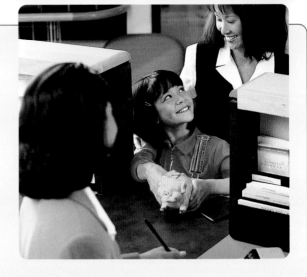

A Word About MONEY

Long ago in Italy, the people who lent money sat on benches. That's where they did all their business. The Italian word for bench is banca. The word *bank* comes from banca.

Saving Money for a Long-Term Goal

What if you want to save for college? That is a long-term savings goal. If you are only ten years old, then you have eight years to save. How can you best save during those eight years?

You can buy a CD. A CD will pay you higher interest than your savings account. You will probably have to keep renewing it, however. Most CDs are for a limited time period.

You can also buy a savings bond. You would earn more interest than with a savings account. However, if you cash in your bond before it reaches its full value, you may not make as much money as you would if you left the money in a savings account.

CHAPTER 4

Making and Using a Budget

Are you ready to start managing your money? Then you need to make a plan, called a budget. In your budget, you will record the money that you get, earn, spend, and save.

A budget can help you
- make better use of your money.
- remember what things cost.
- think before you buy something.
- be smart about how you spend money.
- save more money.

I don't have that much money. Do I really need a budget?

Why Budget?

You may be surprised by how much money you get in one year from gifts, allowances, and other sources. You may be even more surprised to find out how much money you spend in one year.

A budget will help you think differently about money, no matter how much you have. You'll learn to plan ahead. A budget will help you make your money work for you!

How can I set up a budget that will work for me?

Getting Started

To set up a budget, you need to think about

- how much money you receive or earn.
- how much money you spend each week or month.
- how much money you want to save.
- what you would buy or do with the money saved.

Setting Up a Budget

Here's how a budget works. Cassie gets an allowance and does chores around the house. Sometimes, she also earns money helping people in her neighborhood. Cassie hasn't been able to save any money, and she wants to buy a guitar. She does not know where all her money goes. So she asks her parents for help setting up a budget. Here are the steps she followed.

Step 1: List ways to get money.

Cassie began by listing all her sources of income for one week.

Allowance
Household chores
    Dust, clean room
    Wash dishes
Mother's helper

She wrote down the money she earned in one week.

Money Earned

Allowance	$5.00
Dust furniture 2x/week	$4.00
(2 x $2.00 = $4.00)	
Be mother's helper	$5.00
for Mrs. Grossman	
Total	$14.00

Whenever Cassie spent money, she jotted down how much she spent. At the end of the week, she looked over her figures.

Money Spent

Movies	$5.00
Pizza/Soda	$2.90
Snack	$.75
Snack	$1.25
Magazine	$3.20
Total	$13.10

Then she subtracted the amount she spent from what she earned. That's the money she had left to save, 90 cents.

Cassie kept track of the money she earned and spent over the next few weeks. She realized that it would take forever for her to save enough money to buy a guitar. So she looked for ways to spend less and save more.

Looking over her budget, she saw that she was spending too much money on snacks. She decided that one way she could save money was to bring snacks from home.

Cassie also realized from her budget that she needed to find other ways to earn money. Cassie decided that she would see if another family in the neighborhood needed a mother's helper.

Over the next few months, Cassie's budgeting helped her reach her goal. She saved enough to buy a guitar. Now she needs to save for guitar lessons!

Kids Take Action

You can use the money management skills you learned not only to help yourself but to help others as well. You can use your skills to make a difference in your community. Many kids donate their time and raise money for causes that matter to them.

What can you and your friends do to raise money for your community?

Here are some things that you and your friends can do to give back to your community.

- Organize a group that collects money for the United Nations Children's Fund (UNICEF) at Halloween. The money goes to help children around the world who have little food and are sometimes homeless.

- Raise money for Habitat for Humanity International®. This group builds houses for families in need.

- Hold a fundraiser to help the American Red Cross. This organization helps families in countries torn by war or ruined by floods, tornadoes, earthquakes, or other natural disasters.

How can you help your own community?

Kids Plan to Raise Money

Mrs. Hanover's class is studying how new homes are built. The students find out about an organization called Habitat for Humanity. Volunteers come from all over. They pound nails, paint, or do whatever the builders tell them to do. In no time, a family who could not afford to buy a home has a brand-new home.

Mrs. Hanover's class wants to raise money for this organization. The money will be used to buy house-building supplies.

How will Mrs. Hanover's class raise the money?

Mrs. Hanover's class has been studying businesses. They decide to split into groups to form a small company. The company will make three different products. The class takes a survey of the kinds of products kids might buy from them. They **poll,** or ask, other classes. The class discovers that kids are most interested in products for themselves, such as hair items, jewelry, or school supplies.

Over the next few weeks, the kids brainstorm product ideas. They come up with three products. The products are hair clips, braided bracelets, and book covers. All will have the word Habitat on them. The kids will sell these items at lunch and after school.

What kind of business could you and your friends start to raise money?

Class Project: Business Plan

1. Choose one of three products to develop.
2. Work out a product budget. How much money is needed to buy supplies? What is a fair price to charge?
3. Make sample products.
4. Advertise products in the school and in the community.
5. Sell products.
6. Keep track of sales and costs.
7. Donate profits to Habitat for Humanity.

To raise money to donate to an organization of your choice, you need to develop a plan. This plan will help you reach your goal.

Step 1: Identify a goal.

- Discuss organizations in your town to which you would like to give money.
- Decide if you would rather give to a well-known national or to an international organization, such as UNICEF.
- Know why you want to donate to the organization you choose.

Model

Mr. Jackson's class decided to form a business that would donate its profits to a charity. The class reviewed a number of different charities. They decided on the Red Cross. In social studies and science, they learned about natural disasters, such as hurricanes and tornadoes. They learned that the Red Cross helps people after disasters strike.

Step 2: Decide on a business.

- Decide if your business will make a product or offer a service.
- If you choose to make a product, what will it be?
- If you decide to perform a service, what will it be?
- How will your product or service make money for your charity?

Model

Mr. Jackson's class brainstormed ideas for making money. They wanted to start a business that helped others. Some wanted to have a car wash. Others wanted to make and sell food. Still others wanted to provide a service that would help younger children. Mr. Jackson's class noticed that many parents needed help with their children after school. Funds for the after-school program had been cut. The class voted to start a Help Kids company. They would care for and tutor children after school.

- Decide how the business will be organized and run. Assign tasks.
- Decide what prices to charge for the service.
- Decide how much time each person will spend on the business.
- Prepare an advertising campaign to promote the business.

Model

The class held meetings to determine hourly rates for tutoring and baby-sitting. They decided that each student would give two hours a week to the business. They decided to advertise their services and tell people what their profits would be used for. They would send notes home to the parents. They would post ads on community bulletin boards.

The class planned to be in business for one month. The business proved to be so successful that it was still going on after two months.

Determine how often you should get together to report profits, solve problems, and make suggestions to improve the business.

Model

After the first financial report was given, Mandy asked for ideas for handling difficulties with one small child. Two or three other kids reported activity ideas that everyone could use when they baby-sat. The preschool director talked to them about what interested small children. By the end of the session, the group had come up with a list of activities to keep small children occupied.

The class learned how to run a business, manage money, and give back to their community. After running the business for three months, Mr. Jackson's class gave the Red Cross $250.

Glossary

allowance an amount of money given regularly

barter to trade by exchanging goods or services for other goods or services without using money

budget to plan how to spend your money

certificate of deposit (CD) a type of bank savings plan in which a set amount of money is deposited for a specific period of time at a fixed rate of interest

charge to put off paying for something until later by using a credit card or signing an agreement

check a written order directing a bank to pay a certain amount of money

competitive comparable in price to similar items

credit trust in a person to pay a debt later

goods items that are sold

interest a charge that is paid for the use of borrowed money

invest to use money to buy something that will make more money

mature to reach full value

minimum the least possible amount of a bill that must be paid

penalty a fee that must be paid for withdrawing money before a set date

poll to ask for the opinions of others

portfolio a group of different stocks

profit amount of money left over after the costs of operating a business are subtracted from the money earned

prototype the first version of an invention that tests an idea to see if it will work

savings account money that earns interest while kept in a bank

savings bond a certificate issued by the United States government for a loan of money

service a job or task that a person does for other people

statement a monthly report that tells how much money plus interest are in a bank account, or how much money is owed on a credit card

stock shares in a company

textile having to do with making cloth

Index

advertising 15, 30
allowance 11, 13, 24, 25
bank 19-20, 22
barter 6
budget 13, 23-25, 28
business
  plan 28-30
  product-oriented 16-17, 28
  service-oriented 14-15, 29
certificate of deposit (CD) 20, 22
checks 9
child labor 12
credit cards 9, 10
interest 10, 19, 20, 22
money
  coins 7-8
  different forms of 6-8
  earning 11-17, 24, 25, 28-30
  history of 6-8
  paper 7-9
  raising 26-30
  saving 18-22, 23, 24, 25
  spending 5, 10, 13, 23, 24-25

pricing 14, 16, 17, 28, 30
profit 17, 28, 29, 30
savings account 19, 20, 22
savings bond 20, 22
selling 11, 15, 16, 17, 28
stocks 21
supply and demand 16
United States Mint 8
wampum 7, 8